Jack and the Beanstalk

Maggie Moore and Steve Cox

W
FRANKLIN WATTS
LONDON • SYDNEY

Once upon a time there lived a boy
called Jack. He and his mother were
very poor.

"We don't have enough to eat," said Jack's mother. "We will have to sell the cow to buy some food."

So Jack had to take the cow to market.

On the way to the market they met a strange little man.

"That's a fine cow you have," said the man. "Will you sell her to me?"

"Yes," said Jack gladly. "How much will you give me?"

6

"I'll give you five beans," replied the man.

"Five beans!" gasped Jack. "That's
not enough."

"Aah, but they are magic,"
the man smiled.

Jack accepted the beans and took them home to his mother.

Jack's mother was very annoyed.

"You silly boy," she cried crossly.

"Those are not enough even for one
meal. We will still be hungry," and she
threw them out of the window.

But the beans were magic. During the
night they grew and grew.

When Jack looked out of the widow he saw the beanstalk reaching high into the sky.

"Wow!" gasped Jack.

"I'm going to the top."

He climbed and climbed until there

was no more beanstalk left and then

he saw ...

... a huge castle. He tiptoed to the gates then wriggled inside through a gap under the door.

Jack explored the enormous room.
Suddenly, the floor began to shake and
Jack heard an ear-splitting voice.

"Fee, fi, fo, fum, I smell the blood of an Englishman," it roared.

"Be he alive or be he dead, I'll grind his bones to make my bread."

16

It was a giant! Jack was terrified.

He ran to a cupboard to hide.

He peeped out and watched horrified
as the giant ate five whole sheep for
supper. Then the
giant called
his hen.

"Lay, hen. Lay!" he roared.

The hen quivered and then laid a perfect

egg made of gold. Jack was amazed.

Eventually the giant fell asleep.
Jack crept out of the cupboard
and across the floor.

He quickly picked up the hen and put
the golden egg in his pocket.

He edged towards the door, but the hen began to squawk and flap her wings. The giant woke up.

He banged the table with his fists.
"Fee, fi, fo, fum, I smell the blood of an
English man," he roared.

Jack held tightly on to the hen and
raced back to the beanstalk. He
scrambled down as fast as he could.

But the giant chased after him.

"I'll get you," he yelled.

He began to climb down the beanstalk,
but he was clumsy and slow.

Jack reached the bottom. He picked up his axe and chopped down the beanstalk while the giant was still near the top.

The giant fell down with such a huge

thud that the ground shook.

That was the end of him!

The hen was very happy living with Jack and his mother and laid a golden egg every day.

"Thank goodness for magic beans,"
Jack thought.
"We will never be poor again!"

About the story

Jack and the Beanstalk is a British fairy tale. The earliest version appears in 1807 but it is an older story than this. The best-known version was told by Joseph Jacobs in his *English Fairy Tales* in 1890. Joseph Jacobs was born in Australia in 1854, and came to England when he was 18 years old. He edited many fairy tale collections. He wanted English children to be able to read English fairy tales as well as those from France and Germany, which were already popular.

Be in the story!

Imagine you are Jack's
mother when she sees
the beanstalk
outside her
window.

What will
you say to
Jack? Will you
still be cross or
will you forgive him for
selling the cow after all?

First published in 2014 by
Franklin Watts
338 Euston Road
London
NW1 3BH

Franklin Watts Australia
Level 17/207 Kent Street
Sydney
NSW 2000

A CIP catalogue record for this book is available
from the British Library.

The artwork for this story first appeared in
Leapfrog: Jack and the Beanstalk

ISBN 978 1 4451 2827 6 (hbk)
ISBN 978 1 4451 2828 3 (pbk)
ISBN 978 1 4451 2830 6 (library ebook)
ISBN 978 1 4451 2829 0 (ebook)

Series Editor: Jackie Hamley
Series Advisor: Catherine Glavina
Series Designer: Cathryn Gilbert

Printed in China

Franklin Watts is a divison of
Hachette Children's Books,
an Hachette UK company.
www.hachette.co.uk